D1308931

Computers

Brian Williams

Heinemann Library
Chicago, Illinois

© 2002 Reed Educational and Professional Publishing
Published by Heinemann Library,
an imprint of Reed Educational & Professional Publishing,
Chicago, Illinois

Customer Service 888-454-2279
Visit our website at www.heinemannlibrary.com.

Designed by Tinstar Design
Originated by Ambassador Litho
Printed by Wing King Tong in Hong Kong/China

06 05 04 03 02
10 9 8 7 6 5 4 3 2 1

Library of Congress Cataloging-in-Publication Data
Williams, Brian, 1959-
  Computers / Brian Williams.
    p. cm. -- (Great inventions)
  ISBN 1-58810-210-6
  1. Computers--History--Juvenile literature. [1. Computers--History.]
I. Title. II. Series.
  QA76.23 .W55 2001
  004'.09--dc21
                              2001000107

Acknowledgments
The author and publishers are grateful to the following for permission to reproduce copyright material:
Cover photographs: Dixons, Photodisc, and Science Photo Library.
p. 4 Jerome Yeates/Science Photo Library; p. 6 Hutchinson; pp. 8, 9, 10, 12, 14, 19, 23, 30, 36 Science Museum/Science & Society Picture Library; pp. 16, 18, 27 David Parker/Science Photo Library; p. 20 Bettmann/Corbis; p. 21 Hulton Getty/Keystone; p. 22 REPP; pp. 25, 34, 41 Edward Holub/Corbis; p. 26 Trevor Clifford; p .28 Peter Newark; p. 29 Maxmillan Stock Ltd./Science Photo Library; p. 31 Rosenfield Images/Science Photo Library; p. 32 NASA/Science Photo Library; p. 37 Stone; p. 38 Photodisc; p. 39 Robert Harding; p. 40 Oxfam; p. 42 Tek image/Science Photo Library; p. 43 Sam Ogden/Science Photo Library.

Every effort has been made to contact copyright holders of any material reproduced in this book. Any omissions will be rectified in subsequent printings if notice is given to the publisher

Some words are shown in bold, **like this.** You can find out what they mean by looking in the glossary.

A note about dates: in this book, dates are followed by the letters B.C.E. (Before the Common Era) or C.E. (Common Era). This is instead of using the older abbreviations B.C. (Before Christ) and A.D. (*Anno Domini*, meaning "in the year of our Lord"). The date numbers are the same in both systems.

Contents

Introduction

Computers are as important in the twenty-first century as steam engines were in the nineteenth century. They may change our lives more than any other invention of the last 2,000 years. All over the world, people use computers for work and for playing games, to study and find information, to buy things, and to send messages to friends.

One person did not invent the computer. Different parts were invented at different times, and the computer is still evolving. It is a machine that mimics the human brain—it can remember, think, and learn. The brain is still the best computer there is, but only time will tell how far computers will be developed.

Why do we use computers?

The first computers did calculations more quickly than a person could and without making mistakes. A computer can deal with huge amounts of information, or **data,** performing millions of calculations every second. Even more useful, computers can be programmed, or given sets of instructions to follow. Computers can fly planes, control factories, guide spacecraft, and run stores and banks. Many aspects of modern life depend on them.

Modern home computers, such as the Apple iMac, are small, easy to use, and amazingly powerful for work, playing games, e-mail, and Internet communications.

Computers are **digital.** This means they use numbers. A digit was originally a finger, useful for counting on. Numbers were invented at least 5,000 years ago, long before there were computers. People invented numbers to keep records to answer questions such as, "how many," "how far," and "how much?" We use numbers when doing mathematics, and math helps us to make sense of the universe.

The computer revolution

For thousands of years, people did all their counting in their heads or in written form. Traders used counting machines, such as the abacus. No one needed to calculate faster than a bead could be pushed along a wire.

About 400 years ago, scientists tried to make machines to calculate difficult math problems. The first calculating machines had wheels and levers and added up only as fast as the wheels turned and the levers clicked. Unlike humans, they did not get tired of doing the same calculations over and over again. Unfortunately, they could not do anything else.

Advances in electronics brought about the first computers in the 1940s, but the computer revolution really began in the 1970s, when computers became small enough to sit on desks or fit on laps. Computers moved out of the laboratory and into stores, schools, offices, and homes.

The story of computers has chapters on many inventions, from the abacus to the **microchip.** To begin the story we must go back 3,000 years, to some pebbles in the sand.

How a computer works

Computers hold some data in their internal memory and take in new data from their external memory. The computer's "brain" is the central processing unit, or CPU. Input is data fed into the computer. Output is what comes out.

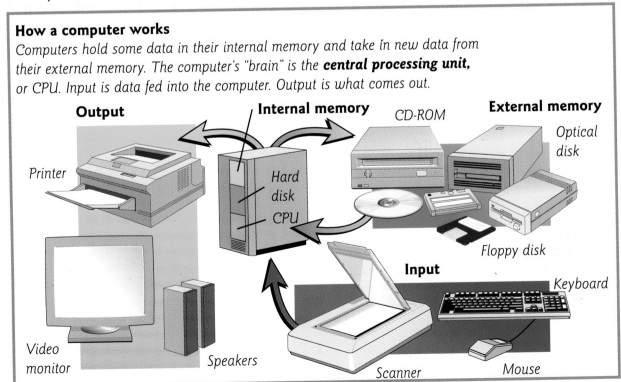

Output · Internal memory · CD-ROM · External memory · Optical disk · Printer · Hard disk · CPU · Floppy disk · Input · Keyboard · Video monitor · Speakers · Scanner · Mouse

The Abacus, 3000 B.C.E.

Nobody knows when people started to count, but we can be sure they counted on their fingers. The Aztec and Maya people of central America counted by 20s using both fingers and toes, but counting by 10s was more common.

Learning to count

About 10,000 years ago, groups of people became farmers and built the first cities. Farmers grew crops and kept herds of sheep, goats, and cattle. They needed to know how much each farmer owned. They made scratches on stones and trees or made piles of stones, one for each animal. They kept records of how many sacks of grain they sold by cutting notches on sticks. Some sticks were split down the middle so the buyer and seller could each have a record of the deal.

In the age of the pocket calculator, some people still use the abacus, sliding beads more quickly than most of us push buttons.

The Babylonians, Chinese, and Egyptians invented writing and number signs. They made marks, like notches—one mark for 1, two for 2, and so on. Around 3000 B.C.E., someone invented the first calculating "machine," the abacus.

The dust machine

The abacus was invented in Babylon in what is now Iraq and used all over the ancient world. The name abacus comes from a Hebrew word meaning "dust." The first abacus was a block of wood sprinkled with dust on which figures were written with a stylus, or pointer. People also arranged pebbles as counters, arranging them on a wooden board in rows to stand for ones, tens, hundreds, and so on. To make counting quicker, abacus boards either had grooves for the pebbles to rest in or had beads strung on rods or wires. About 3,000 years ago, the Chinese invented a two-part abacus called a *suanpan.*

The *suanpan* had nine or more vertical wires with beads strung in columns. The first column on the right stood for "ones," the next for "tens," then "hundreds," and so on, so a nine-wire abacus could count up to hundreds of millions. A dividing bar separated the upper and lower sections. The upper section had two beads on each wire, and each bead represented five units. The lower section had five beads on each wire, and each lower bead represented one unit. Beads were moved up or down to the dividing bar when doing calculations.

Traders and shopkeepers in Asia continued using the abacus until the late 1900s. It could add, subtract, divide, and multiply, and an abacus expert could do calculations faster than a mechanical calculator!

Modern numbers

Numbers evolved gradually. The Egyptians were writing signs for numbers as long as 5,000 years ago. Modern numbers come from signs written in the 300s B.C.E. by Hindus in India, improved by Arabs, and copied by Europeans. Indian mathematicians invented the zero, which was written as a dot at first. The Romans, who had their own number system, never had a zero, which made Roman calculations tricky. Without the Indian-Arab numbers 1–9, mathematicians could not have invented mechanical calculators. Without another form of numbers known as **binary code,** invented in the 1600s, no electronic computers would work as fast as they do today.

8000 B.C.E.	3000 B.C.E.	3000 B.C.E.	1000 B.C.E.	100 C.E.	800s C.E.
People became farmers and began keeping records.	The first written numbers are invented in the Near East.	The Babylonians invent the abacus.	The Chinese invent the *suanpan,* or 2-section abacus.	Roman numerals are used throughout the Roman empire.	Hindu-Arabic numerals reach Europe.

Slide Rule, 1621

Before 1600, all calculations were done either with an abacus, by writing out calculations on paper, or in the head. Difficult calculations took a long time. Engineers, shipbuilders, and house builders relied mostly on guesswork and experience when pencil and paper calculations proved too difficult.

Napier's logarithms

In 1614, a Scottish mathematician named John Napier **published** a set of tables, which he called logarithms. The mathematics are difficult to explain, but the tables were easy to use and made multiplying long numbers twice as fast.

Logarithms made it possible to do multiplication by adding. Take the following as an example. The bottom line of numbers are logarithms, or "logs," like those worked out by Napier.

Numbers	1	2	4	8	16	32
Logarithms	0	1	2	3	4	5

To multiply two numbers from the top line, say 2 x 4, look in the bottom row. Under 2 is log 1 and under 4 is log 2. Adding 1 + 2 makes 3 and above log 3 is the answer to the sum: 8.

Logarithms were especially useful for machine-calculators because machines can add more easily than they can multiply. Logarithms were quickly put to practical use in the slide rule.

Early slide rules were round, like clock faces. By the 1800s, people were using slide rules that looked more like rulers with sliding sections.

The first slide rule

Around 1620, an English astronomy professor named Edmund Gunter suggested that Napier's logarithms could be used in a "pocket calculator" or slide rule, though he did not actually make one. Gunter was interested in measuring—he invented the surveyor's chain, a 100-link chain 66 yards (20 meters) long. In 1621, an English mathematician named William Oughtred made the first slide rule, as Gunter had suggested, but he told very few people about it. He was a scientist, not a workman, so he didn't realize how useful it was.

The slide rule was a thin, numbered ruler slotted inside a wider ruler. To use it, you slid the rulers to line up a figure on one ruler with a figure on the other, and read the answer. Handy slide rules were on sale by the 1650s and were soon in the toolboxes of most carpenters, stone masons, shipbuilders, and architects.

Almost every engineer knew how to use a slide rule until the 1970s, when electronic calculators and computers replaced slide rules for most jobs. The biggest slide rule, used by a U.S. aircraft maker in the 1950s, was the size of a table!

Inventors argue
Oughtred took twelve years to publish his invention and then became involved in an argument with one of his students, Richard Delamain. Delamain made his own slide rule in 1630, three years before Oughtred made his invention public. It was circular, not ruler shaped. Even so, Oughtred felt that a rival had stolen his idea. Angrily, he accused Delamain of disloyalty, though it is possible that Delamain figured out the slide rule for himself.

John Napier (1550–1617)
Napier went to study at a university when he was 13, but did not graduate. He became a mathematician but spent much of his energy involved in religious argument, writing many letters to the king. He found time to invent weapons such as burning mirrors and armored chariots, as well as logarithms, which he hoped would be useful to astronomers. Napier invented a method of multiplying and dividing by using rods. It came to be known as "Napier's bones," because the rods were made of bone or ivory.

"Napier's bones" were a set of rods which could be used for multiplying and dividing. They were packed in a handy carrying case.

1614	1620	1621	1859	1886	1890
In Britain, John Napier invents logarithms.	English astronomer Edmund Gunter suggests using logarithms in a slide rule.	Mathematician William Oughtred invents the slide rule but keeps it to himself until 1633.	The first "modern" slide rule is invented by Amedee Mannheim of France.	The first white, plastic slide rule is produced.	A double-sided slide rule is invented by William Cox of the United States.

Calculator, 1623

A calculator is a small electronic keypad that helps us do calculations. Its seventeenth-century ancestor was a very different kind of machine.

The first calculator could not have been invented without clockwork. Mechanical clocks date from the thirteenth century, but they were not very accurate until the addition of a **pendulum** in the mid-1600s. Clockwork contained a complicated arrangement of the toothed wheels and springs needed to make a machine that could do calculations—a mechanical calculator.

The first calculators

The first calculator was made by a German inventor named Wilhelm Schickard in 1623. It combined logarithms with linked gear wheels. These were the basis for clockwork, but they went back thousands of years to the first waterwheels. Schickard's machine looked like an old-fashioned cash register, and it could do multiplication and long division.

This is a 1960 copy of Schickard's 1623 calculating machine. It was made from the original drawings and proved that the German inventor's machine worked.

Schickard never got the credit he deserved for his invention. A later machine, made in 1642 by the brilliant young French scientist Blaise Pascal, is often said to be the first calculator. His machine had a set of gear wheels connected to dials. To work it, you entered numbers using the numbered gear wheels. Pascal's machine could handle up to eight columns of figures, but adding was really all it could manage.

Leibniz's bright idea

The trouble with both these machines was their slow speed. Even an average mathematician could often do the same calculation more quickly than the machine. Slow as they were, the machines showed what might be possible, given a more "machine-friendly" arithmetic. Between 1666 and 1679, the German mathematician Gottfried Wilhelm Leibniz worked on a way of counting based on **logic,** in which 0 could stand for "false" and 1 could stand for "true." Leibniz had invented **binary code,** the number system now used by all computers.

Leibniz also tinkered with Pascal's calculator, and in 1694 he made a better machine that could multiply and divide. Called the "Stepped Reckoner," it worked in "steps" by repeated additions, like a modern computer. It was not reliable, so the calculator remained a scientific toy. Life still moved at a slow pace. People did not yet need a machine that could compute faster than a person could think.

Binary code

The binary number system was the work of the German scientist-philosopher Gottfried Wilhelm Leibniz. "Binary" comes from a Latin word meaning "two at a time." Binary arithmetic is based on 2, not 10. It uses only two digits, 0 and 1, which have different values according to their position. For example, in binary code, the numbers 1 to 10 look like this:

Base 10	Base 2 (Binary)			
	8	4	2	1
1				1
2			1	0
3			1	1
4		1	0	0
5		1	0	1
6		1	1	0
7		1	1	1
8	1	0	0	0
9	1	0	0	1
10	1	0	1	0

Leibniz had come up with the perfect number system for computers, but no mathematician of his own time could see much use for it. Today all computers use binary code, with electrical pulses flicking on and off at an amazingly fast speed.

1092	1623	1642	1656	1666-1679	1694
Chinese scientists build a water-powered astronomical clock.	Wilheim Schickard of Germany builds the first mechanical calculator.	In France, Blaise Pascal invents his calculating machine.	The first pendulum-regulated clock is made by Christiaan Huygens of Denmark.	German Gottfried Wilhelm Leibniz suggests binary code as a new way of counting.	Leibniz invents a calculator he calls the "Stepped Reckoner."

Punched Card, 1805

What is the link between a computer and a **loom** for weaving tapestries? The answer came about in the late eighteenth century. In 1790, a French engineer named Joseph-Marie Jacquard was trying to make textile weaving more efficient. The workers operating weaving machines had to follow very complicated patterns and made too many mistakes.

Weaving by using cards

French inventor Jacques de Vaucason had tried to speed up silk weaving by using cards with guide-holes to **program** the hooks that carried the silk, so every thread was woven into the right pattern. To change the pattern, the weaver put in a new card with a different arrangement of holes.

Jacquard invented his punched-card programming system to control weaving looms like this one, which had 400 needles. It was constructed in Spitalfields, London, in 1810.

Jacquard worked to improve the punched card arrangement. He "translated" each textile pattern into a code of holes on card. Each card let a needle make correct stitches but blocked the needle if it tried to make a wrong stitch. This "yes/no" principle was the forerunner of the "on/off" principle of **binary code,** later used in the electronic computer.

Workers revolt

The French Revolution interrupted Jacquard's inventing. For a time he went to war, fighting on the side of the revolutionaries. When peace returned, he went back to work, and by 1805 he had finished his punch card loom. By feeding in a new set of cards, the weaver could alter the pattern being woven. Jacquard had invented the first programmable machine.

However, it was not a good time to introduce such an invention. France was soon at war again, and workers were not ready for new ideas. When Jacquard tried to set up his new machines in a factory at Lyon, the weavers rioted. They were afraid that they would lose their jobs, like the home workers in England who had been replaced by new spinning machines. Jacquard escaped harm, but had to watch his new looms go up in flames.

The punched cards survive

Fortunately, the French government took up his idea. They awarded Jacquard a state **pension** and paid him a **royalty** for each machine he made. Punched card looms were soon in factories across France. The punched card would play an important part in computer history in the 1830s, when English inventor Charles Babbage tried to build a revolutionary computing machine.

1789	1790	1805	1806	1812	1830s
The French Revolution begins.	Joseph-Marie Jacquard works on his new loom.	Joseph-Marie Jacquard perfects his punched-card loom.	The French government takes over the Jacquard loom.	While Napoleon is invading Russia, there are 11,000 Jacquard looms at work in France.	Charles Babbage uses punched cards in his plans for a revolutionary computing machine.

Babbage's Computer, 1835

In the early 1800s, during the **Industrial Revolution,** Britain was called the "workshop of the world." Charles Babbage, professor of mathematics at Cambridge University, was a man of ideas. He helped found the Royal Astronomical Society and the **Statistical** Society. He invented a speedometer and a cowcatcher, a device for clearing the track in front of steam trains. In 1835, he invented the world's first **digital** computer.

Babbage's engines

Babbage spent much of his time using long mathematical tables. He dreamed of a machine that could do calculations quickly, helping scientists and engineers. He spent his life trying to build a giant computer.

Babbage's Difference Engine No. 1 had toothed wheels marked with decimal numbers.

His first attempt was a machine he called the Difference Engine. By turning a handle, he could make it perform calculations. Babbage was not satisfied and planned a much bigger machine, the Analytical Engine. This had the main parts of a modern computer: memory, control unit, and **programming** using punched cards, like those pioneered by Joseph-Marie Jacquard in France. These cards would "weave" numbers instead of thread. The Engine would be able to compare quantities and make decisions based on the result of the comparison. It would also change its own program and print out its results.

> ## Ada, Countess Lovelace (1815–52)
> The daughter of the poet Lord Byron, Ada was brought up by her mother, Annabella Milbanke, after her father left England. It was from her mother that she got her love of numbers. Bored by fashionable parties, she was more interested in going to science lectures. She met Charles Babbage, and the two became lifelong friends. In 1835, Ada married the Earl of Lovelace and they had three children. She went on helping Babbage with the programming and design of the Analytical Engine.

An engineer's nightmare

Babbage worked on plans for this machine for 40 years, but never saw it completed beyond a crude first stage. The Engine was an engineer's nightmare, a giant jigsaw of gear wheels, levers, and pulleys. Despite the pioneering work of Hans Oersted and Michael Faraday in the 1820s, electricity was still little more than a toy. Babbage lived in a world of gaslight and steam engines, and without electricity and electronics, his computer remained a dream.

The first programmer

Babbage was helped by Ada, Countess Lovelace. She wrote the first punched-card programs for Babbage's dream machine. She was a remarkable mathematician who combined work on the first computer with the life of an English gentlewoman.

1805	1820–21	1835	1859	1871	1937
Joseph-Marie Jacquard uses punched cards to program a **loom.**	Hans Oersted and Michael Faraday describe electromagnetism.	Charles Babbage describes his analytical engine.	Englishman George Boole describes a **logic**-based algebra, the theory behind the electronic computer.	Charles Babbage dies and his computer is forgotten.	Charles Babbage's plans are rediscovered.

Census Counter, 1890

The first official, national **census** in the United States was in 1790. Censuses were taken every ten years, and the task got bigger as more and more citizens filled in more answers to more questions.

The census problem

This mass of **statistics** had to be sorted. A national census produced so much information that it took practically until the next census to sort out the **data.** The government could use this information to determine how much tax money it would get or how many new schools should be built.

*Herman Hollerith's tabulator looked a bit like an upright piano. Metal pins opened and shut an electrical **circuit** to count data.*

Hermann Hollerith was in the numbers business. A young statistician, he began working for the U.S. Census in 1880 and saw how much work was involved in sorting by hand. Hundreds of workers sat checking the census forms. In 1884, Hollerith was asked by his boss to come up with a better system for analyzing the data from the 1890 census. It was estimated that to count just three sets of these figures (a person's sex, birthplace, and job) would take 100 clerks seven years. Could it be done faster?

The tabulator

Hollerith devised a machine called a tabulator which dealt with the figures by sorting them by category and counting. He used punched cards, similar to those in the Jacquard **loom.** He also borrowed ideas from Babbage's Difference Engine, which he had read about. The new tabulator processed the 1890 census returns in six weeks.

Business machines

By 1901, the tabulator had been improved. Data was recorded in number **code** by a typist who used a special keyboard to punch holes in cards. The holes represented numbers and were counted electrically using metal pins that passed through them and made contact with a tray of mercury underneath. Every time this happened, the electrical circuit was completed. The tabulator could count several kinds of data at once.

Hollerith's machines were soon being bought by businesses. By the 1920s, workers in offices, many of them women, were employed on tabulators and similar machines.

Herman Hollerith (1860–1929)

Hollerith studied at the Columbia University School of Mines and was recruited by his teacher to work on the 1880 census. While teaching, experimenting with air brakes, and working in the **Patent** Office in Washington, he continued to work on a machine that would speed up the census. His tabulator, with punched cards in which the position of the holes represented numbers, attracted great interest among business people. Hollerith's Tabulating Machine Company, set up in 1896, later grew into the computer giant International Business Machines Corporation (IBM).

1868	1880	1890	1896	1920s	1960
Thomas Edison invents a push-button vote recorder for Congress, but they don't want it.	Herman Hollerith works on the U.S. census.	The first machine-sorted census using the tabulator is conducted in the United States.	Herman Hollerith sets up a tabulating machine company.	Businesses are buying Hollerith's machines.	Census returns begin to be analyzed by computer.

Electronic Tube, 1904

Until the 1950s, all radios had "tubes," which glowed and needed time to "warm up." These airless tubes were the keys to the radio and electronic revolution of the 1900s. In 1883, Thomas Edison, then the greatest inventor in the United States, was puzzled by the glow he saw inside his most famous invention, the light bulb. He was puzzled because the glow came not from the heated wire inside the glass bulb but from the apparently empty space around it. What was going on?

Inside the tube

While experimenting with **vacuum tubes,** scientists like William Crookes in Britain observed that as an electric **current** passed along the tube, from one metal **electrode** to another, the tube glowed brightly.

In 1897, British scientist Joseph Thomson showed that inside vacuum tubes, streams of electrically charged particles, called **electrons,** were being given off by the negative electrode, or cathode. These were cathode rays. Vacuum tubes would be crucial to the invention of radio, television, and computers. They could create electronic signals, make them stronger, mix them, or separate them.

Lee De Forest is pictured here holding his Audion vacuum tube. A brilliant inventor, he was a poor businessman, selling his **patents** *cheaply.*

The diode

Radio began in 1895 with the first experiments in "wireless" telegraphy by Guglielmo Marconi. One of the scientists who helped Marconi was John Ambrose Fleming. It was Fleming who in 1904 made the first radio tube. Called a diode because it had two parts, or electrodes, it could change **alternating current** (AC) to **direct current** (DC). It controlled a flow of current and it could pick up radio waves.

The triode

In 1906, the American engineer Lee De Forest invented an improved vacuum tube called the triode. It had three parts: two electrodes plus a wire grid. A weak signal flowing to the grid could control a much larger current between the two electrodes. The triode was the first **amplifier**—it could make signals stronger so that radio broadcasts could be heard much more clearly over long distances. The triode could also "switch on" or "switch off" a flow of electrons. This made it possible to build the first computers using **binary code.**

Listening to the radio at home became part of family life in the early 1900s, thanks to the invention of the vacuum tube.

De Forest called his triode tube an Audion. He sold it in radio kits for people to build at home. In 1910, he used it for the first outside broadcast in the United States. Radio listeners heard the Italian opera star Enrico Caruso sing "live" from the Metropolitan Opera House in New York City.

Until the 1950s, vacuum tubes were used in all radios, radar devices, and televisions. Vacuum tubes were also used in the first electronic computers of the 1940s, such as ENIAC (Electronic Numerical Integrator Analyzer and Computer). No computer could work without them until the transistor was invented.

Electromagnetism and radio

In 1865, British scientist James Clerk Maxwell suggested that invisible forms of energy travel through space. Further work by the German scientist Heinrich Hertz, who discovered these **electromagnetic waves** in 1886, led to the invention of the radio. The first radio signals were sent in 1895 by Guglielmo Marconi. This was the beginning of wireless communication— the **telegraph** in 1837 and the telephone in 1876. Both relied on signals passing along wires.

1865	1879	1895	1897	1904	1906
James Clerk Maxwell puts forward the idea of invisible electromagnetic waves.	In Britain, William Crookes invents a vacuum tube to study cathode rays.	The first radio signals are sent by Guglielmo Marconi.	Joseph John Thomson discovers electrons and receives a **Nobel Prize** in 1906.	John Ambrose Fleming invents the diode vacuum tube.	Lee De Forest invents the triode, an all-purpose electronic device.

Electronic Computer, 1939

By the 1930s, experimental computers were being built in the United States. Mathematician George Stibitz, working on telephone systems for Bell Laboratories in New York, realized that "on-off" signals could be used to turn telephone switching equipment or even lights into machines for doing arithmetic. He invented a machine he called the Complex Number Calculator.

At a university in Iowa, physicist John Atanasoff was working on a more advanced machine, using a special kind of **logic** called Boolean logic. A primitive version was ready in 1939, but World War II halted work on a second model, which had 300 **vacuum tubes** and used punched cards to input **data.** It would have been the first electronic computer to use **binary code.** A Harvard University team led by Howard Aiken built a **"digital** adding machine," the Mark I. It took six years, from 1937 to 1943, but it was not all-electronic and it could do fewer tasks.

ENIAC

Presper Eckert and John Mauchly worked together to build ENIAC, the first all-electronic computer.

By 1946, another American team, led by Presper Eckert and John Mauchly, had built a better machine. ENIAC (Electronic Numerical Integrator Analyzer and Computer) weighed 27 tons (30 metric tonnes) and had 18,000 glowing vacuum tubes to do the "on-off" switching done by telephone switches in the Mark I. It used so much electricity that when it was switched on, the lights around the University of Pennsylvania dimmed!

ENIAC could calculate 1,000 times faster than a mechanical calculator. It was built to calculate the flight of shells fired from artillery guns, doing calculations in two hours that would have taken 100 engineers a year. The slowest part was programming the machine. The problem of how to store **programs** in a computer so it could reprogram itself if necessary was a problem solved by the mathematician John von Neumann.

BINAC and UNIVAC

ENIAC was followed by BINAC (Binary Automatic Computer), the first stored-program computer in the United States. In 1951 UNIVAC (Universal Automatic Computer) was built. UNIVAC could work with letters as well as numbers, and it had separate input and output systems.

UNIVAC startled everyone by predicting the result of the 1952 presidential election. Analyzing data from opinion polls and earlier elections, it forecast General Dwight D. Eisenhower to win easily. Not believing the machine, scientists reprogrammed UNIVAC because they thought there was a fault somewhere. Eisenhower won the election, beating Adlai E. Stevenson by more than six million votes.

In the 1940s, computers had no transistors or integrated **circuits.** This meant they were big machines with lots of wiring on large circuit boards. Changing a program usually meant rewiring the circuits.

John von Neumann (1903–57)

Hungarian-born John von Neumann was a brilliant mathematician. He studied in Berlin, Zurich, and Budapest and came to teach in the United States in 1930. His interests included physics, math, climatology, games, flight, and computing. His work on computer logic and memory helped make electronic computers more accurate and more able to program themselves.

1859	1939	1946	1946	1946	1952
Englishman George Boole showed that step-by-step logic can be reduced to simple "on-off" sequences.	In the United States, John Atanasoff builds an electronic digital calculating machine.	ENIAC is the first electronic computer that can do more than one task at at time.	First use of the term "bit" by engineers working on ENIAC. Bit stands for "**Binary digit.**"	At the University of Pennsylvania, Presper Eckert and John Mauchly invent BINAC.	Eisenhower wins the presidential election, just as UNIVAC predicted.

Colossus, 1943

During the early twentieth century, new "computing machines" were invented to solve more difficult engineering and military problems. The outbreak of World War II in 1939 brought rapid progress as the **Allies** battled to outwit the Germans and Japanese in a secret scientific war.

Computers in the 1930s

In 1930, an American engineer named Vannevar Bush built a machine to do complicated calculations using changes in electrical **voltage** to represent numbers. Bush's "Differential Analyzer" was used to solve difficult problems, such as figuring out the best shape for an aircraft wing to allow air to flow easily around it.

The Germans were also trying to build an electrical calculating machine. In 1938, Konrad Zuse built a computer that was very fast for its time, but slower than a pocket calculator of today. Zuse wanted to build a bigger machine, but the **Nazi** government in Germany said no, preferring to spend money on planes and tanks.

The German army and navy used Enigma machines to code top secret messages. Enigma altered the code from day to day.

Computers at war

When World War II began, both sides tried to intercept enemy radio messages sent in **codes** based on letters and numbers. The Germans used coding machines that could automatically alter the code from day to day. To read enemy codes, the British tried using a **primitive** computer to analyze the long strings of numbers making up intercepted messages, but it kept breaking down. In 1943, Tommy Flowers, a telephone engineer, got a call from Alan Turing, one of Britain's most brilliant scientists. Turing was a top code-breaker, and he asked Flowers to help design a computer that could break the German codes.

Colossus and the Enigma variations

The new machine, named Colossus, began to run in December 1943 at the British code-breakers' headquarters, Bletchley Park. It was tested by a problem that took 30 minutes to solve. Working nonstop for four hours, the machine gave the right answer eight times.

By good luck, the Allies had captured a German Enigma coding machine, which looked like a typewriter with sets of numbered wheels. Colossus now had the key to unravel the German secrets. The computer raced through the millions of possible settings for Enigma's numbered wheels and was able to read every message radioed by the Germans and picked up by the Allies.

A second Colossus machine hummed into action five days before the Allies invaded France on June 6, 1944. By the end of the war in 1945, there were 10 machines at work, 24 hours a day. The computer had helped shorten the war and saved many lives.

Alan Turing (1912–1954)

British mathematician Alan Turing was a pioneer of computer theory. In 1936, he described what scientists now call a "Turing Machine"—a computer that could be **programmed**, store **data**, and process it step by step. Turing worked in the United States before returning to Britain during World War II to help break German secret codes. After the war, he helped build Britain's first electronic computers. Turing believed that one day a computer would be capable of thinking.

1930	1936	1938	1943	1944
Vannevar Bush builds the differential analyzer.	Alan Turing describes computer principles in the "Turing Machine."	Germany almost takes the lead in computers with Konrad Zues's Z-1, the first programmable calculator.	The first British code-breaking computer, the Colossus Mark 1, is made.	Colossus Mark II reads codes to help the Allies liberate occupied Europe in World War II.

Operators work the Colossus computer in 1943 at Bletchley Park.

Transistor, 1947

By 1948, engineers had succeeded in building computers with small memories that could be **programmed** by **primitive** software. These first computers could hold one or more sets of results in their memories for use in other, more difficult calculations.

The first computers were huge. Only government departments and college laboratories had the room and the staff to run a computer, especially since the thousands of **vacuum tubes** inside them constantly "blew." It was common for tubes to blow and stop working after only eight minutes! A more effective device was needed to replace the tube.

Solid state breakthrough

In 1947, three engineers working at Bell Laboratories came up with the answer. William Shockley, Walter Brattain, and John Bardeen had studied materials called **semiconductors,** which were neither **conductors** of electricity nor **insulators.** They found that semiconductors conducted **current** in two ways, which they called n-type and p-type. "N" stood for negative and "p" for positive. N-type contains mostly negative-charge carriers, and p-type contains mostly positive-charge carriers.

This discovery was the clue to a new kind of device, the transistor. Transistors are solid state devices—the signals in them flow through a solid but not through a vacuum. The best semiconducting material was found to be **silicon.**

How a transistor works

A transistor has three parts, called the base, collector, and emitter. When no current flows in the base, almost no current flows between collector and emitter. But when a small current flows in the base, a big current can pass between collector and emitter. So a transistor can control a big current with a small one.

base — collector — no current — emitter

base — small current here — collector — current flows — even bigger current: transistor fully on — emitter

Like a triode, the transistor worked both as a switching device and an **amplifier,** by changing electrical **resistance.** It could control a big current while using only a tiny current itself, and it could open or close a **circuit** in a millionth of a second. The first transistor was more than .5 inch (10 millimeters) long, but within four years, much smaller ones were being made.

The transistor revolution

Transistors were cheap and easy to make. Because they were so much smaller than vacuum tubes, transistors could be fitted into handy-sized devices, such as pocket radios and hearing aids. Smaller computers, no longer taking up whole rooms, began to appear in schools, offices, and homes. Transistors were an important step in this miniaturization revolution, and around the corner was the amazing world of the integrated circuit.

For their invention of the transistor, Shockley, Brattain, and Bardeen received the **Nobel Prize** for Physics in 1956.

The transistor could do the same job as a vacuum tube, but was much smaller and used less power. The first transistorized computers appeared in the late 1950s.

1947	1953	1954	1958	1959	1960s
John Bardeen, Walter Brattain, and William Shockley invent the transistor.	Transistors are fitted into hearing aids.	The first mass-produced silicon transistors go on sale.	Seymour Cray designs the first all-transistor computer.	IBM sells its first transistorized computers.	Transistors replace vacuum tubes in radios, and portable transistor radios become popular.

Floppy Disk, 1950

The first computers were not easy to use. Each time they wanted the machine to do something different, **programmers** had to reconnect hundreds of wires. This took a long time, and it was easy to make mistakes.

Speeding up the functions

All **digital** computers have the same basic functions—input, storage, control, processing, and output. In the first computers of the 1940s, **data** was stored on large drums of magnetic tape, and tape was still being used into the 1970s. Punched cards were widely used to input data.

In 1955, there were only 250 computers in the world. If home computing was to catch on, a simple data-store was needed. The answer came in the shape of a plastic rectangle, the floppy disk.

A floppy disk can store all of the words for one of these books. A computer hard drive stores many times more data on a stack of magnetic disks.

The disk drops on the desk

The floppy disk was invented in 1950, but it was not designed for computers. It was a magnetized disk for storing information in the form of electrical signals. Its Japanese inventor, Yoshiro Nakamata, who claimed to have **patented** more than 2,000 other inventions, sold his idea to the computer giant IBM. In 1971, IBM engineers produced their first computer disk. It held only 100 kilobytes of data within a plastic case just 3.5 inches (90 millimeters) square. Modern floppies hold 1.4 megabytes, or about 3 million text characters.

Inside the disk

The modern floppy disk does not bend. The flexible part is a plastic disk with a magnetized coating that is protected from dust and damage by a tough plastic case. The floppy disk made computers much simpler for people to use. All they

had to do was put a floppy into the computer's disk drive, and the computer "read" the information on the disk. Floppies could also be used to store new information "saved" from the computer's hard disk. The data on a disk is recorded as electrical signals. Magnetic sound recording, pioneered in the late 1800s, had been developed into tape players in the 1930s. Converting this technology to make the floppy disk, and later the compact disc, brought about a huge increase in computer use. By 1980, there were more than one million computers, and the number has been growing ever since.

In the 1960s, magnetic tape on reels was used to input and store computer data. The floppy disk revolution made computers smaller and easier to use.

Magnetic Forces

Magnetism is the force that one electrical **current** has on another current. Certain materials, such as lodestones (known to the Ancient Greeks) are natural magnets because of the way their **electrons** move. This mysterious force was first studied by William Gilbert of England in the early 1600s, but not fully understood by scientists until the 1800s. The first experiments in magnetic sound recording were made in the 1890s and led to the invention of the tape player in the 1930s. Modern magnetic storage systems, like the floppy disk, built on these earlier discoveries.

1898	1936	1950	1959	1961	1970s
Valdemar Poulsen of Denmark records sounds on a wire, a **primitive** form of magnetic recording.	The German magnetophone is the first tape recording system.	The floppy disk is developed in Japan and later developed for computers in the United States.	IBM sells its first transisterized computers.	The term "byte" is first used. One byte represents a character (letter or number).	Floppy disks are used in the first personal computers.

Robots, 1952

In the 1950s, people became interested in robots, partly because scientists were interested in **automation,** and partly because of a craze for science fiction movies. The aliens and robots in these movies were usually actors inside uncomfortable costumes!

The rapid progress in computers and **artificial intelligence** led to experimental machines that could be taught and could learn to change the way they worked. Computer-controlled robots could replace people for dangerous work, such as handling radioactive material in nuclear plants or venturing into deep space.

Factory robots

Robots could also replace human workers in factories. Henry Ford had started building cars on assembly lines in the early 1900s, long before there were computers. Now assembly line work could be done by "intelligent robots," machines that would never get bored or tired.

In 1952, scientists at the Massachusetts Institute of Technology built the first machine tool that was electronically **programmed.** Four years later, American engineer George Devol invented a mechanical arm that could be taught to do simple tasks. His partner, Joseph Engelberger, fitted the arm to the first computer-controlled factory robot.

At the Ford car factory in 1910, each car body moved along the assembly line as workers added wheels, engines, seats, and so on. It was faster than building one car at a time.

Robots on the job

Devol and Engelberger sold their first "Unimate" robot to a car plant in 1962. Fifty robots could do the work of 200 human welders assembling car bodies. The Japanese were quickest to put hundreds of computer-guided robots to work, speeding up car production in their factories. Today, thousands of robots work all over the world.

These robots are at work in an assembly plant. The robot worker is taught its job by a computer that memorizes the actions required and then programs the robot to copy them.

Intelligent robots have electronic sensors that act as "eyes," "ears," and "feelers." Their "brains" can react to changes and reprogram the machine. Some robots are amusing toys and others have more serious tasks. Army robots disarm terrorist bombs. Other robots patrol museums at night, like robot guard dogs. Most robots move on wheels or tracks, though some have legs. Smart robots look for the nearest electrical socket to plug into when their batteries need recharging.

The robotic mouse

In 1938, an engineer named Thomas Ross built a mechanical mouse. There had been many mechanical toys before, some driven by clockwork, others by steam or electricity. Ross's mouse was unusual. It ran on toy train tracks and was programmed never to repeat a wrong turn. If it ran up a dead end, it avoided that turn on its next run. The mouse was one of the first machines to learn from experience.

1954	1962	1980	1980s	1990	1997
The first **patent** for a robot arm is granted.	The first industrial robot, the "Unimate," goes to work in the United States.	The Puma Robot, produced by Unimation, Inc., has more skills. It can tighten nuts.	Japanese car companies put hundreds of robots to work on car assembly lines.	Bell Laboratories' SAM is the first speech-activated robot, able to understand voices and talk back.	The Sojourner robot lands on the surface of the planet Mars.

Integrated Circuits, 1958

The first electronic **circuits** were large boards into which wires, tubes, and other parts were plugged or stuck. For computers to become really convenient, circuits had to be much smaller. The transistor provided the answer.

Make it smaller!

Engineers tried to fit more and more transistors onto smaller and smaller circuit boards. The result was the integrated circuit or IC, made by an American named Jack Kilby, who worked for Texas Instruments. The idea for a solid-**silicon** "microchip" had been suggested in 1952 by a British inventor named Geoffrey Dummer but was not pursued. In 1958, Kilby put together a number of transistors and **capacitors** on a single base using a microscope to see the miniature parts. He **patented** his invention in 1964.

Integrated circuits were soon being used in a new generation of computers, as well as in guided missiles, space satellites, and other machinery. They helped make possible the high-tech moon landing in 1969.

Integrated circuits are very small, less than .25 in. (4 mm) square, but can store thousands of bits of information.

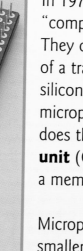

The marvellous microprocessor

In 1971, Intel engineers designed the first "computer on a **chip**," the microprocessor. They chemically fixed all the tiny components of a transistor onto a single wafer, or slice of silicon. The media called it a microchip. The microprocessor chip is an "intelligent" unit that does the same tasks as the **central processing unit** (CPU) of a much bigger computer. It has a memory and can be **programmed.**

Microprocessors made it possible to design smaller, more powerful computers that could be assembled inexpensively in factories. Smart chips were soon being used in many other devices, such as store cash registers, television sets, navigation equipment, factory robots, and cars.

Small is better

The secret of the microchip was its size—"micro" is a Greek word meaning small. In the first microchip, one transistor sat on a surface less than one-fourth of an inch (seven millimeters) square. Today, thousands of components are present on one tiny paper-thin chip. The chip works fast because signals have such tiny distances to travel.

The microscopic circuits are planned on a table-sized board, one layer at a time. Then a miniaturized version, or mask, is made photographically from the final master layout. From this mask hundreds of chips can be made on one silicon wafer. A single chip can store more than five million bits, or units of information.

Circuit designers plan a new circuit on a large master board. The finished circuit will be a photographically exact miniature of the master.

Intel and Silicon Valley

Robert Noyce, who worked with Jack Kilby on the integrated circuit, was one of a group of young computer "whiz kids" who set up business in the 1960s and 70s in California's hi-tech inventions zone, later known as Silicon Valley. His company, Intel, grew and grew and by 2000 it made the most widely used computer chip in the world, the Pentium. Chips seldom fail. If one does, it is simply replaced with a new one.

1958	1971	1976	1986	1990s	1990s
In the United States Jack Kilby builds the first itegrated circuit using **semiconductor** material **soldered** to thread-like wires.	The first microprocessor, the Intel 4004, is invented.	The first commercial supercomputer, the CRAY I, is built. It has 200,000 integrated circuits.	First **graphics** processors make computers more "user-friendly."	Very large scale integration (VLSI) circuits have more than 100,000 transistors.	Single chips store about five million bits and perform 100 million instructions per second.

Virtual Reality, 1960s

In the 1960s, using computers much less powerful than today's, the first virtual reality simulators were designed to train pilots. Jet planes are too fast and too expensive to be entrusted to inexperienced pilots, so a trainee pilot relied on the simulator. Within an artificial visual world of land, sea, and sky, the trainee "flew" faster than sound without ever leaving the ground. Multimedia brings together the magic of television, video, sound, and computers. Virtual reality goes even further, using computers to simulate real life or to create worlds that look real.

Conjuring up unreality

Virtual reality, for education or entertainment, can seem magical to people who are unfamiliar with the power of computers. It was impossible before the development of computer **graphics programs.** These are so powerful that they can create realistic images—dogs that look like dogs, people that look like people, and monsters that look really scary!

In the 1990s, computer power improved so much that you can now enter a virtual world through your computer. Exploring with your mouse, the computer creates sequences of images so fast that what you see looks incredibly real. You can access these worlds through the Internet or from a CD-ROM. Virtual reality systems can recreate a lost world, such as a Roman arena, and fill it with a roaring crowd of spectators, none of them real. It can create new worlds of fantasy. The images can be shown on a flat screen, in an arcade game, in a movie theater, or on television.

Exploring a virtual world

For even more lifelike effects, the person exploring virtual reality wears a special headset that projects three-dimensional images onto two small screens in front of their eyes. Wearing the headset and using either a joystick controller or special gloves with feedback sensors in the fingers, the explorer can walk around and move objects within the imaginary world. He or she can fire a fake laser in an amusement arcade or "walk" through a virtual landscape, turning corners and climbing stairs.

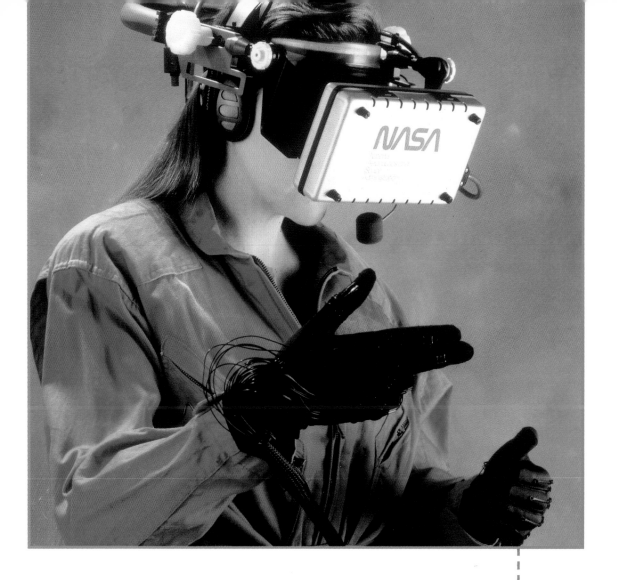

Virtual reality has made computer games more lifelike, and the quality of graphics gets better with each new generation of games. People can now do virtual reality shopping on the Internet. In the laboratory, engineers can simulate crashes to improve car safety features without wrecking a single car. A new plane can be "flown" before a full-size model has been made. Architects can "walk" though a new building and make changes to the design, before the first brick is laid.

Explorers of virtual reality experience imaginary worlds through headsets and special sensor gloves.

1960s	1970s	1974	1989	1991	2000
Flight simulators use video and computers to create the effect of flying while still on the ground.	The first computer games such as *Space Invaders* and *Asteroids* are developed.	Atari's *Pong* is the first big-selling electronic game.	Nintendo introduces the *Gameboy* game system.	The first multimedia PCs with fast graphics and CD readers are developed.	SEGA *Dreamcast* and Sony *Playstation 2* are the most advanced (128-bit) game consoles.

Electronic Calculator, 1960s

The slide rule remained the best instrument for convenient calculations until the 1960s. Then along came the pocket calculator, the "computer in your palm," dreamed up by the inventor of the integrated **circuit** (IC), Jack Kilby.

Working with two friends, Jerry Merryman and James Van Tassel, Kilby was sure the IC could be put into a gadget that anyone could use. They decided to build a mini-computer powered by batteries.

The liquid crystal displays in calculators glow when affected by an electrical current, forming the shapes of letters and numbers.

Japanese designers were at work on the same idea. Their calculator was the size of a small radio but cost ten times as much! Kilby's team knew they could do better, and in 1967 they showed off their hand-held calculator. It had a button keypad and a neat liquid-crystal display. It could add, subtract, multiply, and divide, and although it was bulky, it weighed only 2.2 pounds (1 kilogram).

Where the light comes from

A calculator shows numbers on a small display screen. The glowing numbers are produced either by liquid crystals or by light-emitting diodes (LEDs), which show up better in daylight. LEDs are made of **semiconductor** material coated with plastic. When a **current** passes through the diode, light is given off. LEDs are used in many electronic devices. They are amazingly reliable and, unlike ordinary light bulbs, they seldom fail.

1954	1967	1969	1969	1978	1990s
The solar cell is invented.	Jack Kilby, James Van Tassel, and Jerry Merryman show off their first calculator.	The first scientific calculator is marketed by Bill Hewlett and Dave Packard.	Push-button cash dispensing machines make their first appearance on city streets.	The first **programmable** calculators appear.	Some schools ban students from using calculators, to ensure they learn their multiplication tables.

Bar Code, 1973

Today you see bar **codes** on many packages in stores, but they were unknown before 1973. In 1952 two Americans, Bernard Silver and Norman Woodland, had the idea of using a kind of striped **Morse code** to be read by a light beam, but their idea was not developed. In 1973, Woodland developed the Universal Product Code, the first bar code read by **laser,** while working at IBM.

A bar code is a set of **binary numerals.** The wide bars or spaces stand for 1s and the thin bars and spaces stand for 0s. In a bar code, the arrangement of bars and spaces show numbers or letters. The code can be read backward or forward.

Invisible infrared lasers scan the bar code. At a supermarket, the grocery clerk moves each item over a window and the laser scanner reads the bar code. The store's computer shows the price on the cash register display and adds up the bill. Using bar codes, the computer records every purchase made during the day and keeps track of stock so that the store does not run out of anything.

The laser scanner in the reader is like the laser in a CD player. It fires a beam of infrared light across the code. Only the white spaces reflect the rays. The detector "reads" the beam and converts the on-off pulses into an electrical **binary code** that goes to the computer. A similar technology is used in cards that are "swiped," such as credit cards.

ISBN 0-431-13241-0

9 780431 132419

A bar code is a coded arrangement of bars and spaces. A laser scanner can read the code in one sweep and send the information to a computer.

1952	1960	1974	1980	1990s	1990s
The bar code is first proposed, but there is no laser to make it work.	Theodore Maiman builds the first laser.	A store in Ohio is the first in the world to use a bar code scanner.	IBM and NEC (in Japan) perfect the laser-scanning bar code systems for stores.	Bar codes are used by post offices to sort mail.	Magnetic "swipe" cards, such as credit cards, are in widespread use.

Personal Computer, 1970s

In the 1970s, the computer became a plastic box, packed with power and cheap enough to buy and use at home. In the 1990s, many people could take their computer with them, as a battery-powered **laptop,** for use anywhere.

The PC revolution

The first small-scale computer was the Altair. It was developed in 1974 by a firm called MITS using microprocessors from the Intel Corporation. However, it had to be assembled from a kit, so it didn't appeal to the average person. The personal computer (PC) revolution really began in 1977 when Apple computers, founded by Steven Jobs and Stephen Wozniak, launched the preassembled Apple II. The PC revolution was driven by young inventors such as Jobs at Apple and Bill Gates at Microsoft.

The Apple Lisa, released in 1983, was one of the first home computers, which you could learn to use in less than 30 minutes. It was not around long but helped create demand for even better machines.

The parts that make a PC

At the heart of the PC is its **central processing unit,** or CPU, with thousands of electronic **circuits** all packed onto one **chip,** the microprocessor. The computer screen, or VDU, is basically a television that receives its signals from the computer instead of through cables or an antenna.

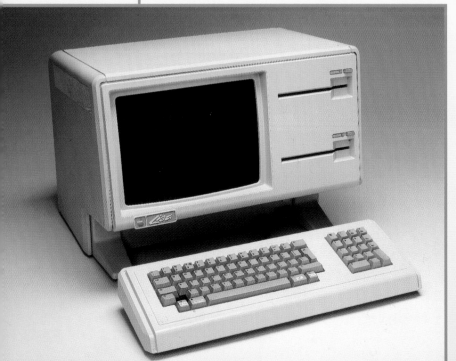

The keyboard borrowed its layout from the typewriter. The typewriter's layout begins with the line of letters QWERTY at the top. The QWERTY arrangement was familiar and most computers still use it. By 1997, there were mini-keyboards, which were smaller than a credit card, but had 64 keys.

The mouse

In 1965, Douglas Engelbart invented the mouse. This allowed people to tell the computer what to do by pointing at icons on the screen instead of using the keyboard. As the mouse rolls around on a ball, the computer tracks the mouse electronically. As the mouse moves, so does the cursor. When the cursor stops over an icon, you can click the mouse button and the command shown by the icon will be carried out.

The mouse was first used on Apple computers in 1983 and adopted by IBM in 1987. For portable laptop computers, developed in the 1980s, the mouse was adapted to a small roller-ball, with fingertip control. Today, some laptops don't have a mouse. Instead, they have an area that is touch-sensitive, which carries out the same function.

The laptop computer was a hit with people who wanted to carry a computer with them or to work from home.

Printers

PC owners wanted to print out work they did on the computer. Dot matrix printers went on sale in 1957. **Laser** printers, which are faster and higher quality, came along in 1975. Starting in 1988, PC users could buy color laser printers.

Bill Gates (born 1955)

Bill Gates was born in Seattle, Washington, in 1955 and became interested in computers in high school. When he was 20, he and his partner, Paul Allen, founded Microsoft, the first personal-computer software company. By the time he was 30, Bill Gates was a billionaire. Microsoft introduced its first Windows software **program** in 1985 and went on to dominate the global market in computer software.

1974	1977	1979	1984	1985	1998
The first home PC, the build-it-yourself Altair with an Intel 8008 microprocessor, is released.	The Apple II computer comes complete in plastic case, with screen, floppy disks, and keyboard.	GUI (**graphical** user interface) allows users to point and click at screen icons with a mouse.	The Commodore 64 was the first best-selling home computer.	Bill Gates launches the first Windows software.	Apple launches the *iMac*, a colorful home computer.

CD-ROM, 1982

The first person to record sound was Thomas Edison, when he spoke into his cylinder phonograph in 1877. In the 1960s, Beatles fans listened to music on vinyl records, tracked by a metal needle running in grooves. The music was recorded by **analog** recording. A copy of the sound waves was stored electrically in the grooves on the disc.

Origins of the CD

In the 1960s, engineers who were tired of scratchy records and worn-out needles, developed a system for recording sound **digitally** onto a magnetic disc. Digital recording turns the sounds into magnetized pulses, which on the aluminum-coated disc look like very tiny holes. A **laser** scans the disc to "read" the pulses. The disc does not wear down, and the sound reproduction is perfect. This was the birth of the compact disc or CD. The audio CD went on sale in 1982.

A compact disc looks smooth but is covered in tiny pits. It stores data digitally as 0s (the pits) and 1s (the flat parts in between).

The CD relied on two scientific discoveries, one ancient and one modern. The ancient discovery was **magnetism,** known since the time of the Ancient Greeks 3,000 years ago and first studied seriously in the 1600s. The modern discovery was the laser, invented in the 1960s.

Disks for computers

The CD could store other kinds of **data** as well as sounds. It could store words and pictures, cramming bookfuls of text onto one disk. This made the CD very useful as a computer-storage device. A CD known as a CD-ROM (Compact Disc Read Only Memory) could store huge amounts of information, such as an entire encyclopedia on one disk.

American engineer James T. Russell invented the digital compact disc (**patented** in 1970). Today, robotic machinery is programmed to produce thousands of CDs at a time.

What is ROM?

Every PC has a built-in stack of magnetic disks called a hard drive to store **programs** and data. Information that the computer needs all the time is stored on ROM (read-only memory) **chips.** The computer has another memory, known as RAM (random-access memory). ROM is like a printed book—the computer can read from it but cannot add new information. RAM is more like a notebook in which the computer can add information, alter it, or delete it if it is no longer needed.

A CD-ROM stores information digitally. When the disk is inserted into the disk drive on the computer, information can be read from it. A CD-ROM can store 1,000 times more data than a floppy disk. However, since it is "read-only" you can't erase the data and "write" fresh information onto it. Computers can also read data from DVDs (digital video discs), which have the added ability to play movies.

1877	1935	1960	1982	1990s	1998
Edison's phonograph is the first sound recording machine.	German company AEG makes the first tape recorder to play magnetized plastic tape.	The laser used to scan compact discs is invented.	The first music compact discs go on sale.	Publishers issue books as CD-ROMs.	The first PCs with DVD disc drives are released.

Internet, 1991

The Internet changed the way people use computers. With millions more users every year, it has become a global network for trade, communication, and information exchange.

Creating the net

Until the 1960s, there was no way of linking several computers, let alone millions. Then two inventors, Paul Baran in the United States and Donald Davies in Britain, working separately, invented "packet-switching." It is a system for converting **data** into packages of information, including the addresses of the person sending it and the person receiving it. The packets could be sent through any number of matching computers.

There are millions of web pages on the Internet, and new ones are appearing all the time.

In 1969, the U.S. Department of Defense linked four computers in a system called ARPANET. The goal was to set up a secure communications system in case of war. Within two years, 23 computers were linked by ARPANET. University researchers linked other computers and began sending one another electronic messages, the first e-mail.

@ Oxfam International – Home Page

Oxfam International

Make a Donation

Programs

About

Get in Touch

Get Involved

News

Useful OI Links:
- About Oxfam International
- Our Strategic Plan 2001-2004
- Emergencies
- Contact your nearest Oxfam
- Drop the Debt

Advocacy

Education Campaign

How the internet works

As systems joined together, they created the Internet, or "net." By the 1990s, millions of people were linking their computers to the net through **modems.** A modem changes signals from the computer into signals that can be sent along telephone lines. Much of the Internet passes at high speed along **fiber-optic cables,** which can carry far more messages than the copper wires used in older phone systems.

Companies called Internet service providers (ISPs) began offering Internet connection to computer owners, and **browsers** such as Microsoft's Internet Explorer and Netscape were installed in new computers for home use. Many businesses, organizations, and individuals started to use the Internet to sell goods, provide information about themselves, or exchange news and views. The information superhighway had come into being.

How people use the Internet

The Internet is not owned by anyone. People use it to bank, shop, watch videos, listen to music, chat to friends, and do research. E-mail and e-commerce (Internet-based business) have grown rapidly, and so has web-casting (broadcasting on the Internet). People can access the Internet from **laptops,** mobile phones, and specially adapted TV sets. No one can foresee the future of this amazingly fast-growing phenomenon.

For people who prefer to surf the Internet in company, the Internet café offers real chat as well as chat rooms. People use the Internet for entertainment, for buying things, for banking and business, to find and provide information, and to keep in touch with friends.

The World Wide Web

In 1989, a young British scientist named Tim Berners-Lee, who worked at an international physics laboratory in Geneva, Switzerland, designed an easier way to access information on the Internet. His idea was to use a browser to link documents from different sources. The browser acts like an electronic pathway, guiding the Internet user to other information he or she might want to look at. This was the start of the World Wide Web, opened to the public in 1991.

1837	1958	1960s	1971	1991	1998
Samuel Morse invents the electric **telegraph,** the first wired communication system.	The computer modem is invented, linking computers to the phone network.	Optical fibers are first used in long-distance telephone communications.	The first e-mail is sent by university researchers.	The World Wide Web is opened to the public.	Web TV allows people to "surf the net" on their televisions.

eBook, 1999

Sometime around 1454, a German inventor named Johannes Gutenberg made the first book printed on a press with movable type. Printing was the biggest revolution in reading since the invention of writing 3,000 years before. After Gutenberg, the book did not change much, but no one knows how computers will change books in the twentieth century.

The book

Gutenberg made the book an inexpensive and convenient way to store information. Even so, the first books were too heavy to carry around, with thick leather covers made to last many years. Paper covers, tried in the 1500s, did not catch on until the 1930s.

The electronic book

The Rocket eBook can be used to read pages on the Internet as well as storing 4,000 book pages.

The eBook can be many books in one. All you need is a small handheld computer reader. You can download several books so that wherever you are, you have a mini-library with you. You can then choose whatever book you like. The *Rocket eBook* can hold 4,000 pages but weighs very little, so it is convenient to carry around.

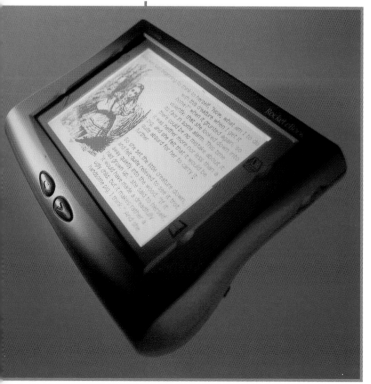

Writers are starting to offer books directly on the Internet. In 2000, thriller writer Stephen King released a new book, *The Plant,* in installments on his website, inviting people to pay him directly for each one they downloaded. He eventually gave up the experiment when he discovered that many people were helping themselves without paying.

The eBook developed from small handheld computers called personal **digital** assistants. They are useful for disabled readers, though not everyone finds them relaxing to read.

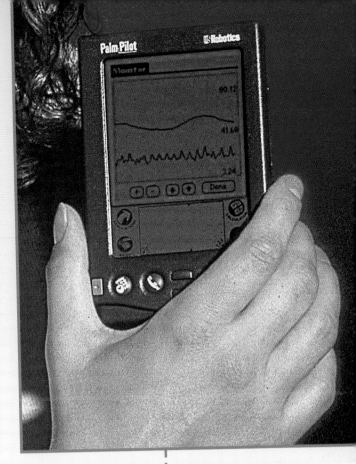

From mouse to eBooks

James Sachs helped design the mouse for the Macintosh computer. He got the idea for his "SoftBook" while flying across the Atlantic in 1996. It can hold the complete works of Shakespeare and comes with a leather cover (like a regular book), a touch-sensitive screen, a page-turner, and a stylus pen, although you can use your finger to highlight text. To download a book, all you do is plug into the nearest phone and go to an on-line bookstore.

One advantage of eBooks is that they cannot be copied. Piracy, or illegal copying, worries publishers and authors. Very popular books are often pirated in printed form within days of being **published.**

The book of tomorrow

The eBook will save on paper, printing, and publishing costs, which account for most of the cost of a book. In the future, a book might never be out of print, but always be available for downloading. The eBook of tomorrow will have not just words, but also film clips, animations, music, and Internet links. The reader might even talk to the book, telling it to go back a page, make the print larger, or read a section aloud!

Palmtop computers are pocket-sized. They can be carried anywhere and can even access the Internet via a phone link. Although these computers are small, they are packed with enough power to do most of the jobs a desktop computer can do.

1930s	1950	1985	1990	1996	1999
Paperback books become popular.	The first computerized speech recognition machine can recognize ten spoken numbers.	The first touch-sensitive screens for computers are developed.	The first computer able to read handwriting, the *Gridpad,* is developed.	The *Palm Pilot* is one of the first pocket-sized readers.	The *Rocket eBook* goes on sale.

Timeline

3000 B.C.E.	The first written numbers are invented in the Near East.
	The Babylonians invent the abacus.
1614 C.E.	John Napier invents logarithms.
1621	William Oughtred invents the slide rule.
1623	William Schickard builds the first mechanical calculator.
1666–79	Gottfried Wilhelm Leibniz suggests **binary code** as a new way of counting.
1805	Joseph-Marie Jacquard perfects his punched-card **loom.**
1820–21	Hans Oersted and Michael Faraday describe electromagnetism.
1830s	Charles Babbage uses punched cards in his plans for a revolutionary computing machine.
1859	The first "modern" slide rule is invented by Amedee Mannheim of France.
	British mathematician George Boole describes a **logic**-based algebra, the theory behind electronic computer development.
1890	The first United States **census** to be sorted by machine is conducted.
1906	Lee De Forest invents the triode, the first all-purpose electronic device that opens the way for the computer revolution.
1939	John Atanasoff of the United States builds an electronic **digital** calculating machine.
1943	The first **code**-breaking computer, the Colossus Mark I, is developed in England.
1947	John Bardeen, Walter Brattain, and William Shockley invent the transistor.
1950	The floppy disk is invented in Japan and later developed for computers in the United States.
1952	The bar code is first proposed, but no **laser** exists to make it work.

1959	IBM sells its first transistorized computers.
1960	Theodore Maiman builds the first laser.
1962	The first industrial robot, the "Unimate," goes to work in the United States.
1969	The first scientific calculator is marketed by Bill Hewlett and Dave Packard.
1970s	Floppy disks are used in the first personal computers.
1971	The first microprocessor, the Intel 4004 is invented.
	The first e-mail is sent by university researchers.
1974	The first home PC, the build-it-yourself Altair with an Intel 8008 microprocessor, is released.
1980	IBM and NEC, a Japanese company, perfect laser-scanning bar code systems for stores.
1984	The Commodore 64, the first wide-selling home computer, is released.
1985	Touch-sensitive screens for computers are developed.
	Bill Gates launches the first Windows software.
1990	The first computer able to read handwriting, the *Gridpad*, is used.
1990s	Magnetic "swipe" cards are in widespread use.
1991	The World Wide Web is opened to the public.
1996	The *Palm Pilot* is one of the first pocket-sized readers.
1998	The Apple *iMac*, a playful and powerful home computer, is released.
	The first PCs with DVD disk drives are released.
1999	The *Rocket eBook* goes on sale.
2000	Sega *Dreamcast* and Sony *Playstation 2* are the most advanced (128-bit) game consoles.

Glossary

Allies people or countries working together with a common goal

alternating current (AC) electric current that changes direction very rapidly

amplifier device for increasing the power of an electrical signal

analog representation of numerical or physical quantities by physical variables such as electrical voltage changes

artificial intelligence ability of a machine to imitate intelligent human behavior

automation making factories in which computer-controlled machines take over certain tasks from people

binary code way of counting based on logic, in which 0 could stand for "false" and 1 could stand for "true"

binary digit digits are numerals 0 to 9. Binary digits are those used in binary code, which use only 0 and 1.

binary numeral number that uses only two digits, 0 and 1

browser program that allows computer users to find things on the Web

capacitor device for storing energy as an electrical charge, usually two metal conducting surfaces with an insulator between them

central processing unit computer's "brain," a microchip that turns the data it is given into a result

census national count of a country's population

circuit complete path taken by an electrical current

code system of symbols or signs used for storing and sending information; a code may be secret or one made for a machine to understand

conductor material through which electrical current passes easily

current flow of electrons along a material acting as a conductor

data information or facts. Data can be processed or stored by a computer.

digital in computers, recording information in number code, or bits

direct current (DC) current that keeps flowing in the same direction

electrode metal plate through which electric current enters or leaves a battery or vacuum tube; either an anode or a cathode

electromagnetic waves form of energy moving very fast through space, ranging in length from short cosmic waves to long radio waves

electron tiny particle inside an atom, which carries a negative electrical charge

fiber-optic cable means of sending data very quickly as pulses of light along thin glass or plastic tubes bundled together

graphics pictures created by a computer

Industrial Revolution social, economic, and scientific changes that began in western Europe in the 1700s, leading to the growth of factories and the use of machines

insulator material that does not conduct electricity or heat

laptop small portable computer powered by batteries

laser device producing a narrow, very focused beam of light

logic form of reasoning used in computer programming

loom machine for weaving cloth

magnetism the force exerted by a magnet, a piece of metal that will attract iron or steel

microchip (or **chip**) tiny piece of semiconductor carrying many electrical circuits

modem device that links a computer to the telephone system, allowing computers to exchange data through the Internet

Morse code system of short electrical signals (dots) and longer ones (dashes) that stand for letters; invented by Samuel Morse

Nazi follower of German dictator Adolf Hitler before and during World War II

Nobel Prize yearly prize for achievement in several areas, founded by Swedish inventor Alfred Nobel

patent description of a new invention, which the inventor presents to a "patent office." No other person can copy the patent without permission.

pendulum swinging weight at the end of a rope or rod, used to control the workings of a clock

pension money paid to someone after retirement

primitive something in an early stage of development

program instructions given to a computer

publish to print something for distribution to the public

resistance fighting against something; a resistor is a material that does not easily let electricity pass through it

royalty payment made to an author or inventor based on how many of their creations are sold

semiconductor material that can behave either as a conductor of electricity, or as an insulator

silicon mineral that is a semiconductor. Wafers of silicon are used to make silicon chips.

solder kind of metal glue (usually a mixture of tin and lead) used to join metals or wires. The solder is melted into place, and hardens as it cools.

statistics numerical facts or the science of collecting and analyzing data

telegraph electrical system for sending messages, invented in the nineteenth century

vacuum tube (also called a valve) airless device used to control the flow of electric current

voltage pressure or "push" of electric current through a circuit

More Books to Read

Casanellas, Antonio. *Great Discoveries & Inventions*. Milwaukee: Gareth Stevens Inc., 2000.

Hoare, Stephen. *The Digital Revolution*. Austin, Tex.: Raintree Steck-Vaughn, 1999.

Sachs, Jessica Snyder. *The Encyclopedia of Inventions*. Danbury, Conn.: Franklin Watts Inc., 2001.

Index